FAITH IN POLITICS?
A TESTIMONY TO EQUALITY

Faith in politics?
A testimony to equality

THE 2017 SWARTHMORE LECTURE

CATHERINE WEST AND ANDY HULL

First published July 2017
Quaker Books, Friends House, 173 Euston Road, London NW1 2BJ
www.quaker.org.uk

ISBN: 978 1 9997269 0 4
eISBN: 978 1 9997269 1 1

Book designed and typeset by Cox Design, Witney
Printed by RAP Spiderweb, Oldham

THE SWARTHMORE LECTURE

The Swarthmore lectureship was established by the Woodbrooke Extension Committee at a meeting held 9 December 1907. The minute of the committee provided for an "annual lecture on some subject relating to the message and work of the Society of Friends".

The name Swarthmore was chosen in memory of the home of Margaret Fell (later Fox), which was always open to the earnest seeker after Truth, and from which Quakers were sent loving words of sympathy as well as substantial material help.

The lecture is funded by Woodbrooke Quaker Study Centre and overseen and supported by the Swarthmore Lecture Committee, which is appointed by the trustees of Woodbrooke. It is a significant part of the education work undertaken at and from Woodbrooke.

The lectureship has a twofold purpose: firstly, to interpret to the members of the Society of Friends their message and mission; and secondly, to bring before the public the spirit, aims and fundamental principles of Friends. The lecturers alone are responsible for any opinions expressed.

The lectureship provides both for the delivery of a lecture, usually at the time of Britain Yearly Meeting of the Society of Friends, and for its dissemination, usually in the form of a book. A lecture related to this publication was given by Catherine West on Monday 31 July 2017 at Yearly Meeting Gathering of the Religious Society of Friends (Quakers) in Britain, held at the University of Warwick.

The Swarthmore Lecture Committee can be contacted via the Clerk, c/o Woodbrooke Quaker Study Centre, 1046 Bristol Road, Selly Oak, Birmingham B29 6LJ.

www.woodbrooke.org.uk/swarthmorelecture

WOODBROOKE
WWW.WOODBROOKE.ORG.UK

QUAKERS

In memory of Jo Cox
(1974–2016)

ACKNOWLEDGEMENTS

We would like to acknowledge and thank a number of individuals for their contribution to the work that went into this book. Martina Weitsch and Tim Newell from the Swarthmore Lecture Committee have been exceptionally supportive with their time and their advice. Sandra Berry made possible an invaluable retreat at Woodbrooke Quaker Study Centre and Simon Best there helped with our communications, as did Anne van Staveren at Friends House, London. The inimitable staff of the House of Commons Library answered our various questions as impressively and obligingly as ever. Anna Gorrell and Nathalie Spells in Parliament took care of all of the complicated logistics with their usual grace. Finally, Ann Morgan, Tony Crofts and Shaun Rafferty kindly hosted Catherine's visits to Quaker-inspired initiatives tackling inequality around the country.

CONTENTS

INTRODUCTION:
EQUALITY AS AN ARTICLE OF FAITH

I am honoured, as the 110th Swarthmore Lecturer, to follow in 2017 in the footsteps of Esther Mombo and her colleague Cécile Nyiramana, whose powerful lecture *Mending broken hearts, rebuilding shattered lives: Quaker peacebuilding in East and Central Africa* I had the privilege to hear at Britain Yearly Meeting 2016.[1] In fact, the themes of our two lectures are connected. Esther spoke memorably of healing a divided community, riven by inequality, that had turned in on itself. There is ample evidence to suggest that countries that exhibit high levels of inequality between groups are more likely to experience violent conflict than more equal countries.[2] When inequality gives rise to such conflict, the violence in turn can compound intergroup inequality, creating a vicious cycle. In recent years, inequality between countries may have diminished, but inequality within countries has increased.[3]

In their bestselling book *The Spirit Level*, Richard Wilkinson and Kate Pickett advance the thesis that inequality is bad for everyone, not just the poor.[4] They show how, as the rich get richer and the divide grows, everybody suffers through social ills such as higher mortality rates, more suicides, worse mental health, more crime, and more people in prison. The subsequent film *The Divide* illustrates powerfully just how arid and isolating life can be for those at the top of an unequal society.[5] Accordingly, reducing inequality benefits everyone.

It is not just how low the bottom is that matters but how big the

1 E. Mombo and C. Nyiramana, Swarthmore Lecture 2016: *Mending broken hearts, rebuilding shattered lives*. Available to download from *SoundCloud*, https://soundcloud. com/swarthmorelecture/swarthmore-lecture-2016-mending-broken-hearts-rebuilding-shattered-lives, accessed 27 March 2017.
2 Institute for Public Policy Research, *Shared destinies: Security in a globalised world* (London: Institute for Public Policy Research, 2008), www.ippr.org/files/images/media/ files/publication/2011/05/Security%20Commission%20Interim%20Report_1666. pdf?noredirect=1, accessed 27 March 2017.
3 Ibid.
4 R. Wilkinson and K. Pickett, *The Spirit Level: Why equality is better for everyone* (London: Penguin, 2010).
5 K. Round, dir., *The Divide: What happens when the rich get richer?* [film] (London: Dartmouth Films, 2015).

gap between the bottom and the top is. Alleviating absolute poverty is certainly important, but reducing relative poverty matters as well. That a child in Kenya can't afford shoes is lamentable, but that she should have to watch her peers in their new trainers every day makes it harder still. It is bad that there is a postcode in the London borough of Tower Hamlets with the lowest average earnings per resident of anywhere in the country. But what makes it worse is that the same postcode has the highest average earnings per employee who works there, in the gleaming towers of Canary Wharf.

As Quakers, we believe in 'that of God in everyone'. In my view, what George Fox meant with these words in 1656 is that every life is both equal and holy. In 1948, the same sentiment found secular expression in the first article of the Universal Declaration of Human Rights: "all human beings are born free and equal in dignity and rights".[6] The recent film *The price of fairness* showed that children develop a strong sense of fairness – or "inequity aversion" – very early on in life.[7] At school, reading George Orwell's allegorical masterpiece *Animal Farm*,[8] they immediately clock the hypocrisy of the ruling pigs' maxim "all animals are equal, but some animals are more equal than others". A commitment to fair process is hardwired into us as human beings. An egalitarian conviction is therefore central to my worldview as a politician in Britain today. Unfortunately, merely believing that all people are created equal does not make it so. Therefore, for me, alongside other Quaker values such as simplicity and sustainability, actively advancing the cause of equality is both a political imperative and a spiritual vocation.[9] This commitment to social justice has driven me on my Quaker journey, though I remain as yet in its foothills.

My own lived experience has taught me how unequal our society can be, but also how we can by our actions redress the iniquities we encounter. For me, the public flows from the personal.

6   United Nations, *The Universal Declaration of Human Rights* (Paris: UN General Assembly, 1948), www.un.org/en/universal-declaration-human-rights, accessed 27 March 2017.
7   A. Gabbay, dir., *The price of fairness* [film] (London: Sideways Film, 2016), www.sidewaysfilm.com/the-price-of-fairness, accessed 27 March 2017.
8   G. Orwell, *Animal Farm* (London: Secker & Warburg, 1945).
9   See information available at 'So, who are these Quakers anyway?', www.aboutquakers.org.uk, accessed 27 March 2017.

My first love was languages. That led me to work for local authorities among asylum seekers for whom English was not their first language, helping families and young people from war-torn countries to access housing, college and healthcare. I became a caseworker for David Lammy, working in weekly advice bureaux in Tottenham, north London. The stories I heard then are the same stories I hear now in my own constituency surgeries. They are tales of housing need, money worries and poor access to secure employment. I wanted then, and I want now, to see politics address the needs of deprived and disadvantaged communities, to tackle the scourge of low pay and the blight of pensioner poverty.

David encouraged me to become a local councillor, which would draw on my background as a Sure Start volunteer. I spent eight years as leader of the Labour Group on Islington Council. After those eight years, having used our time in opposition to develop a radical manifesto to make our borough a more equal place, my colleagues and I won the local elections in 2010 and began work on the Islington Fairness Commission. We knew the gap between the 'haves' and the 'have nots' creates a disconnect in our communities. We were motivated by what we believed then and have proven since, namely that, with innovative policies and political will, many of these problems can be solved. Others had analysed inequality to death; we wanted to own the problem locally and do something about it.

Ada Salter, a Quaker, feminist and pioneer of ethical socialism, is a hero of mine. She founded the Bermondsey Independent Labour Party in the year in which the first Swarthmore Lecture was given. Later, she wrote:

> Women can effect a great change in the social life of the Metropolis... In the affairs of state is needed the unselfish spirit of the good mother who considers the happiness and well-being of all the members of her household rather than the aggrandisement of some... [treating people] not merely

mercifully and humanely, but in the same way as we ourselves would hope to be treated.[10]

Her words encapsulate the drive that I and many Friends feel to address inequality today.

Let me close this opening chapter with a quotation from John Punshon in *Quaker faith & practice* that really resonates with me. It is from chapter 20, on the source of our strength:

> Ever since I first came among Friends, I was attracted to the testimonies as an ideal… I admired a simplicity, a devotion to equality, and a respect for others… The testimonies are ways of behaving but are not ethical rules. They are matters of practice but imply doctrines. They refer to human society but are about God… [They have] a purpose, and that is to get other people to change, to turn to God.[11]

A commitment to equality is an article of faith. Writing this book, then, is an act of discernment and will, I hope, lead to corporate witness. I hope that you find it resounds with the spirit of faith in action.

---

10 G. Taylor, *Ada Salter: Pioneer of ethical socialism* (London: Lawrence & Wishart, 2016), p. 237.
11 *Quaker faith & practice* (London: The Yearly Meeting of the Religious Society of Friends (Quakers) in Britain, 2013), 20.18.

CHAPTER I

Inequality in the UK and the world today

This book is primarily about tackling poverty and reducing inequality here in the UK, the place where I live, work and practise my faith and politics. I have also, however, endeavoured where relevant to bring to life the wider international context.

In the UK, measures of income inequality are usually calculated with reference to equivalised disposable household income. This measure considers the income of a household as a whole, focusing on disposable income, which means income after tax and benefits, with all their equalising, redistributive effects. The figures are equivalised to reflect differences in household size and composition. Income can be measured either before or after factoring in housing costs. Inequality tends to be more pronounced after housing costs have been factored in, as households at the lower end of the income distribution tend to spend a larger share of their income on housing than higher-income households.

Levels of income inequality in the UK have declined gradually in the past decade, largely because the number of workless households has fallen, though they remain significantly higher than they were in the 1960s and 1970s.[12] There was a small reduction in income inequality in the UK following the 2008 recession. The number of people living in relative poverty (i.e. living in households with an income below 60 per cent of the median in that year) after factoring in housing costs in the UK in 2014/15 was 13.5 million, or 21 per cent of the total population, up 300,000 from the year before. Of these, 3.9 million were children. The Institute for Fiscal Studies predicts that these numbers will increase from 2015/16. Indeed, it recently projected a 50-per-cent increase in relative child poverty between 2014 and 2020 (see Figure 1).[13]

Most of the available data on inequality in the UK[14] is at the national level. We can, however, look at inequality in individual

---

12 Institute for Fiscal Studies, *Working paper W17/01* (London: Institute for Fiscal Studies, 2017), www.ifs.org.uk/uploads/publications/wps/WP201701.pdf, accessed 27 March 2017.
13 J. Browne and A. Hood, *Living standards, poverty and inequality in the UK: 2015–16 to 2020–21* [IFS Report R114] (London: Institute for Fiscal Studies, 2016), www.ifs.org.uk/uploads/publications/comms/R114.pdf, accessed 27 March 2017.
14 National Equality Panel, *An anatomy of economic inequality in the UK* (London: London School of Economics and Political Science, 2010), http://sticerd.lse.ac.uk/dps/case/cr/CASEreport60.pdf, accessed 27 March 2017.

(as opposed to household) earnings at a regional level. Figure 2, for instance, shows the ratio of gross hourly pay at the 90th percentile to that at the 10th percentile by region within the UK, including all employees but not the self-employed.

Figure 1: Relative poverty rates with and without planned tax and benefit reforms, 1997/98 to 2020/21

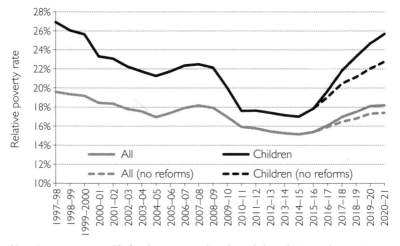

Note: Incomes measured before housing costs have been deducted. Poverty line is 60 per cent of median household income in the current year.
Source: Institute for Fiscal Studies[15]

Despite London, with its unparalleled agglomeration effect, generating more than a fifth of the country's income,[16] the proportion of individuals in relative low income in housing costs in the three-year period from 2012/13 to 2014/15 was higher in London (at 27 per cent) than in any other region, owing to the high cost of housing in the capital relative to other parts of the UK (see Figure 3).

15 Ibid. (Browne and Hood), p. 34.
16 *Mind the gap: London vs the rest* [TV programme] (London: BBC, 2014).

Figure 2: Earnings inequality by region, April 2015: ratio of gross hourly pay at the 90th percentile to the 10th percentile

Region	Ratio
London	4.4
South East	4.1
East	3.9
UK	**3.7**
East Midlands	3.5
North West	3.5
South West	3.5
Northern Ireland	3.5
West Midlands	3.4
Scotland	3.4
Yorkshire and the Humber	3.4
Wales	3.3
North East	3.3

Note: Data are based on where employees live, rather than where they work.
Source: Office for National Statistics[17]

Figure 3: Percentage of the population (all ages) in relative low income, 2012/13 to 2014/15. AHC = after housing costs; BHC = before housing costs.

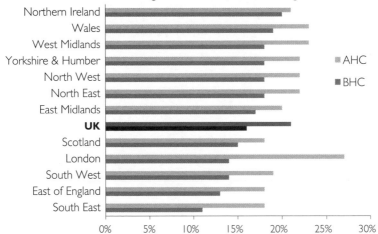

Source: House of Commons Library[18]

17 Office for National Statistics, *Annual Survey of Hours and Earnings, 2015*, www.ons.gov. uk/employmentandlabourmarket/peopleinwork/earningsandworkinghours/bulletins/ annualsurveyofhoursandearnings/2015provisionalresults, accessed 27 March 2017.

18 F. McGuinness, *Poverty in the UK: Statistics* [Briefing paper no. 7096 (14 November)] (London: House of Commons Library, 2016), [p. 26], http://researchbriefings.parliament. uk/ResearchBriefing/Summary/SN07096, accessed 27 March 2017.

These inequalities, especially in the capital, are set to be exacerbated by regressive measures in the Housing and Planning Act 2016, specifically the forced sale of higher-value council homes. It is for such reasons that Victor Adebowale, Chair of the London Fairness Commission, has observed that "there is now a danger that London will become a playground for the super-rich, a treadmill for the middle-classes and a workhouse for the poor".[19]

In terms of international comparisons, figures from the Organisation for Economic Co-operation and Development confirm that income inequality in the UK is higher than in most European countries but lower than in Russia and the United States (see Figure 4).

Academics at the London School of Economics and Political Science have argued that, while the UK's recent decision to opt for Brexit may not exacerbate inequality within the UK, nor will it reduce it.[20] If anything, the result itself of the British EU referendum can be viewed as a response to unfettered inequality and a rejection of those who appeared to defend it. Experts arguing in nine-digit figures and indecipherable acronyms that British membership of the EU was critical to our economy failed to appreciate that too many people felt that same economy was not working for them.

---

19 V. Adebowale, preface to LFC Final Report, London Fairness Commission, March 2016, www.londonfairnesscommission.co.uk/the-london-fairness-commissions-final-report, accessed 27 March 2017.

20 H. Breinlich, S. Dhingra, T. Sampson, and J. van Reenen, 'The distributional effects of Brexit: Who bears the pain?', *LSE Business Review*, 2 June 2016, http://blogs.lse.ac.uk/businessreview/2016/06/02/the-distributional-effects-of-brexit-who-bears-the-pain, accessed 27 March 2017.

Figure 4: Gini coefficients for equivalised disposable income. The data are for 2012, except for Canada and Chile (2011) and Russia (2010).

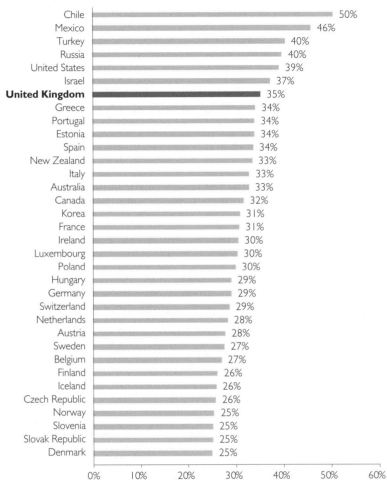

Note: The figures for Russia and Chile are based on a slightly different methodology from the rest of the data.
Source: Organisation for Economic Co-operation and Development[21]

Inequality is at its starkest when viewed globally. As Oxfam has demonstrated, the richest 1 per cent of the world's population

21 F. McGuinness, *Income inequality in the UK* [Briefing paper no. 7484 (4 July)] (London: House of Commons Library, 2016), [p. 20], http://researchbriefings.parliament.uk/ResearchBriefing/Summary/CBP-7484#fullreport, accessed 27 March 2017.

are now richer than the remaining 99 per cent put together, and, shockingly, the richest 62 individuals on the planet have the same combined wealth as the bottom half of humanity, comprising 3.6 billion people.[22] The top skyrocketing and the bottom freefalling are not unconnected. As Alan Krueger and Paul Krugman have explained, the 'Great Gatsby Curve' shows that the higher the levels of inequality in a society, the lower the levels of social mobility.[23] That is to say, inequality of outcome hampers equality of opportunity. In his bestselling book *Capital in the twenty-first century*,[24] Thomas Piketty warns that soaring inequality could lead to political instability.

It is not only progressive academics,[25] civil society campaigners,[26] trade unionists, and social democrats pointing out that inequality has reached dangerous levels. Mark Carney[27] and Andrew Haldane,[28] respectively the governor and chief economist of the Bank of England, have of late criticised levels of inequality in the UK as bad for the country's economic outlook. Similarly, Christine Lagarde, managing director of the International Monetary Fund, has said inequality is leading to protectionism with "tragic" consequences for the global economy,[29] and Gabriela Ramos, chief of staff at the Organisation for Economic Co-operation and Development, has declared that inequality is one of the main obstacles to improved

22 D. Hardoon, S. Ayele and R. Fuentes-Nieva, *An economy for the 1%* (Oxford: Oxfam, 2016), www.oxfam.org/sites/www.oxfam.org/files/file_attachments/bp210-economy-one-percent-tax-havens-180116-en_0.pdf, accessed 27 March 2017.

23 P. Krugman, 'The Great Gatsby Curve', *New York Times*, 15 January 2012, https://krugman.blogs.nytimes.com/2012/01/15/the-great-gatsby-curve/?_r=0, accessed 27 March 2017.

24 T. Piketty, *Capital in the twenty-first century* (Boston: Harvard University Press, 2013).

25 R. Wilkinson and K. Pickett, 'Prepare for the worst: This inequality rift will tear our society apart', *The Guardian*, 3 February 2017, www.theguardian.com/commentisfree/2017/feb/03/prepare-inequality-rift-tear-society-apart-thatcher, accessed 27 March 2017.

26 My Fair London and The Equality Trust, *Why inequality matters* (London: CLASS, 2012), http://classonline.org.uk/docs/Why_Inequality_Matters.pdf, accessed 27 March 2017.

27 BBC, 'Carney warns about popular disillusion with capitalism', *BBC News*, 5 December 2016, www.bbc.co.uk/news/business-38210169, accessed 27 March 2017.

28 BBC, 'BoE's Andrew Haldane warns of regional growth inequality', *BBC News*, 2 December 2016, www.bbc.co.uk/news/business-38186053, accessed 27 March 2017.

29 J. Ewing, 'Inequality is feeding protectionism, IMF chief warns', *New York Times*, 5 April 2016, www.nytimes.com/2016/04/06/business/international/international-monetary-fund-christine-lagarde-inequality-protectionism.html, accessed 27 March 2017.

global economic performance.[30] Put simply, not only is inequality bad in social terms but it hinders economic growth too. The 'trickle-down' economics that US President Reagan asserted in the 1980s have failed: there has been no real increase in US wages in the past 30 years.

Profound economic inequality in the form of disparities in income and in wealth is often accompanied by democratic inequality in terms of imbalances of power and voice. Both forms of inequality contribute to – or rather undermine – important human notions of worth, esteem and respect.

---

30 G. Ramos, 'Inclusive growth: making it happen', OECD Yearbook 2014, www.oecd.org/forum/oecdyearbook/inclusive-growth-making-it-happen.htm, accessed 27 March 2017.

CHAPTER 2

Through politics, progress is possible

Politics is essentially concerned with changing the world around us for the better through dialogue rather than force. It takes two main forms, which are not mutually exclusive and both of which matter: participatory politics and representative politics. The former may range from online single-issue clicktivism to marching on demonstrations to membership of a trade union to organising alongside fellow citizens. The latter tends to mean standing for office or electing others to it. In either incarnation, political activism is a valid route to making change.

Quakers have a rich tradition of such activism, from the 19th-century American Thomas Garrett, who campaigned for the abolition of slavery,[31] to the 20th-century British social reformer Ada Salter, who tackled slum housing in London as one of the earliest female councillors and the capital's first woman mayor. Quakers have fought successfully in Parliament and in their communities for the rights of women,[32] recognition for conscientious objectors, prison reform,[33] offender rehabilitation,[34] conflict resolution,[35] restorative justice,[36] social housing,[37] and support for those who have experienced sexual abuse.[38] Quaker leadership has often been by way of example. The Retreat, for instance, founded in 1792 by Yorkshire Quaker William Tuke, was the first establishment in England where mental illness was regarded as something from which a person could recover and patients were treated with sympathy and respect.[39] More recently,

31 See 'Quakers (Society of Friends)', *The Abolition Project*, http://abolition.e2bn.org/people_21.html, accessed 27 March 2017.

32 See 'Rights of women', *Quakers in the World*, www.quakersintheworld.org/quakers-in-action/166, accessed 27 March 2017.

33 See 'Elizabeth Fry', *Quakers in the World*, www.quakersintheworld.org/quakers-in-action/13, accessed 27 March 2017.

34 See 'Circles of support and accountability in Britain', *Quakers in the World*, www.quakersintheworld.org/quakers-in-action/86, accessed 27 March 2017.

35 See *Alternatives to Violence Project*, http://avpbritain.org.uk, accessed 27 March 2017.

36 See 'Restorative justice', *Quakers in the World*, www.quakersintheworld.org/quakers-in-action/26, accessed 27 March 2017.

37 See *Quaker Housing Trust*, www.qht.org.uk, accessed 27 March 2017.

38 See 'Glebe House: Friends therapeutic community trust', *Quakers in the World*, www.quakersintheworld.org/quakers-in-action/180, accessed 27 March 2017.

39 See 'The Retreat, York, England', *Quakers in the World*, www.quakersintheworld.org/quakers-in-action/92, accessed 27 March 2017.

Quakers have been busting the myths[40] that facilitate rampant economic inequality and developing roadmaps[41] to a more equal society. We can and should draw upon this tradition today. In my own experience as a 21st-century politician, there is every reason to be optimistic about the difference we can make.

What I hope we as Quakers can do is help politicians of all parties and the public to see that tackling inequality should be a systemic priority for the government and for civil society. Inequality has risen in recent decades among democratic countries in the face of very little popular resistance. Despite their achievements in raising the profile of the issue, the 99% and Occupy movements remain outliers. The Nordic model of government, which explicitly seeks to reduce income inequality, remains the exception rather than the rule and is confined to Scandinavia.[42] We need to ask why this is so. Part of the reason may be an excessive credulity when it comes to (often self-justifying) myths of meritocracy and equality of opportunity[43] that assume a level playing field and emphasise the notion of deserts, and a certain denial when it comes to accidents of circumstance. Our society's celebration of success in material terms (developed by the popular media) might also be a contributing factor. A good place for governments to start in terms of tackling corrosive inequality would be the closure of the world's tax havens. The recent film *The UK Gold* contends that the global offshore economy comprises approximately £22 trillion of private wealth, sitting untaxed, primarily in British overseas territories and Crown dependencies and in Luxembourg, while there is £25 billion of tax avoidance in the UK every year.[44]

If established politics, however, fails to address deepening inequality or, worse, is seen to facilitate and endorse it, populism can rise in response – as we saw in 2016. Put bluntly, many people

40 See the section 'Mythbusters' at 'Directory of services: Economic justice', *Quakers in Britain*, www.quaker.org.uk/resources/directory-of-services/economic-justice, accessed 27 March 2017.

41 See the 'Road Maps to Equality' event advertised at *Quakernomics*, www.quakerweb.org.uk/blog/events/road-maps-to-equality, accessed 27 March 2017.

42 Samak, *The Nordic model for dummies* (Oslo: Samak, 2016), www.lo.no/Documents/Engelsk/Nordic%20Models%20for%20Dummies.pdf, accessed 27 March 2017.

43 See 'George Gorman Lecture 2014 – Yearly Meeting Gathering, Bath, UK', *YouTube*, www.youtube.com/watch?v=-HJVUMtoy8o, accessed 27 March 2017.

44 M. Donne, dir., *The UK Gold* [film] (London: Brass Moustache, 2013).

are fed up with having things done to them and being let down by a system that does not feel as if it is designed for their benefit. The result of the referendum on the UK's membership of the EU and the election of Donald Trump as president of the United States are both seismic political ruptures that demonstrate dramatically how, on both sides of the Atlantic, many people consider established politics to be an elite, distant and disempowering affair to which they cannot relate.

We need to address, not dismiss, this profound and prevailing sense of democratic deficit. Politics can give people a stake and a say in the way their society is organised. It can give people a voice. I see it as part of my role to encourage people to re-engage with politics and counter disillusioned detachment. Withdrawal – whether in despair or disdain – simply cedes the political space to forces that would turn us against one another in order to divide and rule, from inflammatory tabloids to racist demagogues. The image that will forever epitomise this problem for me is that photograph of Donald Trump and Nigel Farage together following the former's election to the presidency, grinning in a gold-plated lift – the 'people's champions', supposedly standing up for the ordinary person.[45] And yet, as Quakers, perhaps we should strive to find good in everyone and show love in the face of hatred. Personally, I take inspiration from the example set, for instance, by young Muslim women from the Dialogue Society in Holloway, London, who in December 2016 headed to Forest Hill station to give out roses to commuters in the aftermath of a vicious Islamophobic assault.[46] We have more in common than that which divides us.

.

45 A. Pierce and J. Tapsfield, 'Your gold door's worth more than my house!', *Daily Mail*, 14 November 2016, www.dailymail.co.uk/news/article-3932908/Your-gold-diamond-door-s-worth-house-riotous-inside-story-Farage-s-astonishing-coup-foreign-politician-meet-President-elect-Trump.html, accessed 27 March 2017.

46 H. Collier, 'Muslim volunteers hand out roses at Forest Hill station after "anti-Islamic knife attack"', *Evening Standard*, 14 December 2016, www.standard.co.uk/news/crime/muslim-volunteers-hand-out-roses-at-forest-hill-train-station-after-antiislamic-knife-attack-a3420516.html, accessed 27 March 2017.

CHAPTER 3

Communicating effectively about equality

Polls demonstrate that public support for tackling inequality is widespread but readily trumped by other concerns considered higher priorities, such as economic growth and immigration. Moreover, support among the public for tackling inequality in theory does not appear to translate in practice into support for specific policies that would make the country a more equal place. Focus groups suggest some resignation to the idea that inequality is inevitable. The seemingly popular indifference to profits being privatised while losses are socialised in the wake of the financial crash of 2008 would appear to confirm the findings of this research. Those who campaign against inequality often put excessive faith in the persuasive power of facts, figures and abstract argumentation. It need not be this way. Proponents of equality can and should engage with the particular and the individual, not always operate at the aggregate level; use words and stories, not just numbers and graphs; and speak to people's foremost concerns, for instance by framing inequality as a threat to their children's chances of ever owning a home. Evidence-based policymaking is important, but we need to recognise that evidence comes in many different forms, not just statistics.

There can also be a perceived tension between addressing economic inequality and tackling inequalities according to people's protected characteristics, such as their sex, gender, sexuality, ethnicity, religion or disability. Tackling inequality and tackling inequalities, in this sense, are compatible and can be mutually reinforcing, but it may be helpful to explicitly draw out the relationship between them, for instance by making it clear that winning better wages for cleaners is likely to disproportionately benefit black and minority ethnic women. In the UK, this tension is perhaps more likely to arise when it is Quakers making the case for prioritising economic inequality, since, for now at least, ethnic diversity among Friends remains limited.

There is likewise a potential rub between equality and equity, with the former concerned largely with outcomes and the latter with opportunities. This cartoon sums up the tension well:

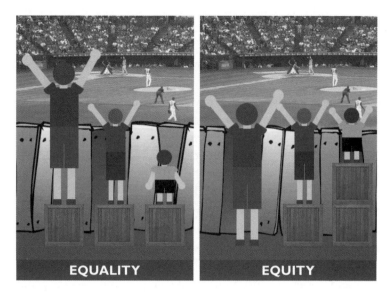

An adaptation of a cartoon by Craig Froehle.

Those at the local level who identify ways to curtail inequality can take action themselves to demonstrate that it is possible. For example, a group of residents from the Butetown area in Cardiff[47] successfully organised itself and lobbied local authorities to tackle the drug problem on their estate and to clean up the needles discarded there. We need such groundbreakers to lead, not plead: not wait for government to catch up, but innovate. Where local change happens, national change can follow. Where it can be demonstrated at a local level that a more equal approach is also a less expensive one, government will show interest, although the standard of cost–benefit analysis required by HM Treasury can be high. Where multiple local actors have the same good idea, they need to team up to make sure they get heard in the sometimes distant corridors of power.

In my experience, there is rarely opposition to reducing poverty at the bottom of the income distribution ('levelling up'), but the same cannot be said of attempts to close the gap by leaning on those at the top of the income distribution ('levelling down'). When I increased the pay of our cleaners as leader of Islington Council, no one argued,

47 R. Flint, 'Butetown: A community taking a stand against drugs', *BBC News*, 24 November 2016, www.bbc.co.uk/news/uk-wales-38025633, accessed 27 March 2017.

but when I stated my intention to finance it by cutting the pay of the role of the chief executive by £50,000, a chorus of naysayers erupted to tell me how we would never be able to find a good chief executive again. Some of these people were recruitment consultants with a vested interest (i.e. a potential percentage commission) in us setting the highest salary possible. Needless to say, having cut the post's pay from £210,000 to £160,000 per annum, we drew an excellent field of candidates and found a first-rate chief executive. If we are to tackle inequality, and not just poverty, then we need to be prepared both to level up and to level down.

CHAPTER 4

We can all make the world around us a more equal place

If we cannot change what is happening on our street, why should anyone believe that we can change the world? Politics starts with the local. There is inequality in all of our communities, so we must begin there, with practical action where it matters, on the ground. If anything, I want this book to be a call to action, to encourage us as Quakers to own the challenge of inequality, offering civic leadership in all our communities.

That is what I tried to do when I established the Islington Fairness Commission as council leader there in 2010. Despite its reputation for wealth and its surfeit of millionaires, Islington is also home to real deprivation. The borough is both poor and unequal:

- it is the 21st most deprived local authority area in England
- it has the highest level of children growing up in workless households in the UK
- it is the most densely populated local authority in the country, cramming 221,000 people into six square miles
- it has the worst health inequalities in the UK for both men and women
- there is a seven-year gap in life expectancy between men in the highest and lowest income brackets
- there is a 10-per-cent gap in educational attainment between the most and least affluent children by the time they leave primary school.

It was against this backdrop that, together with colleagues, I set up the country's first fairness commission to ask how we might tackle poverty and reduce inequality in our part of north London. In a context of swingeing government cuts to the council's budget, residents understood that the commission was about trying to make Islington as fair a place as possible, given the circumstances. I convened 20 commissioners, including not only councillors from different parties but also representatives of trade unions, the NHS, the local college, the police, the chamber of commerce, academics and more. Richard Wilkinson and Andy Hull co-chaired the commission. The idea was that it would shape Islington's agenda, strategy and budget for the years ahead. I wanted it to be both radical and realistic and to show that there are things we can do locally to narrow the gap.

The fairness commission took the shape of a year-long listening exercise. We held seven public meetings around the borough with over 500 attendees, many of them attending more than one session. We sought and heard memorable testimony from local residents, including from 'hard-to-reach' groups. I recall a powerful contribution, for example, from a drug-using sex-worker who recorded an audio piece about her precarious situation, at the mercy of the men she serviced, and her aspiration for a safer life: a room with a hundred people in it sat absolutely silent as that recording played. I remember also a play put on by young people with learning difficulties from the Elfrida Society about their treatment in GPs' waiting rooms, feeling not listened to but spoken down to instead. Authentic testimony like this is powerful because it closes the gaps between people who walk the same streets but inhabit different worlds.

We heard evidence too from expert witnesses, both local and national. We invited and received written submissions from over a hundred local groups and individuals. We set up a cross-departmental problem-solving team of council staff and held bilateral discussions with a wide range of community groups. A crew of policy officers and research staff analysed all the findings. A year later, in June 2011, the Islington Fairness Commission published its final report, *Closing the gap*, containing 19 recommendations to make the borough a fairer place by reducing poverty and inequality in the areas that matter most to people's life chances.[48] Please see Annex A at the end of this book for a list of the commission's recommendations and details of their subsequent implementation.

I shall touch upon some of the many practical achievements to which the fairness commission led in the chapters that follow. For now, though, suffice it to say that it brought huge political benefits too. The fairness commission provided Islington Council with clarity and simplicity of definition: it meant people knew what we were about and what we stood for. It created an Islington brand that has served the borough well ever since. To this day, I am told, applicants

---

48 Islington Fairness Commission, *Closing the gap* (London: London Borough of Islington, 2011), www.islington.gov.uk//~/media/sharepoint-lists/public-records/democracy/qualityandperformance/reporting/20112012/20120303ifcfinalreportclosingthegap, accessed 27 March 2017.

for jobs at Islington Council still turn up at interview explaining how they hope to help make Islington a fairer place. The commission put flesh on the bones of our 'fairness in tough times' mantra, providing a rationale for the tough decisions we had to make. Most of all, though, it enabled us to exercise influence outside our immediate authority, as a convenor and place-shaper.

There have been 31 other fairness commissions across the UK since, ranging from Brighton & Hove, Southampton and Plymouth on England's south coast to Newport in Wales and up to Dundee, Fife and Shetland in Scotland, where the Scottish government has paid close attention to their work. A number of other London boroughs have also played a part in this movement, with fairness commissions to date being set up in Croydon, Greenwich, Redbridge, Lewisham, and Tower Hamlets. In Newcastle, the fairness commission coined an approach to local policymaking known as 'fair share, fair play, fair go, fair say'.[49] In Sheffield, the fairness commission illustrated levels of inequality in the city by charting the journey of the number 83 bus through richer and poorer districts. Most of the fairness commissions so far have been convened by a local authority, but others have been set up by the area's MP, the mayor or a local charity. Many have featured an independent chair or sponsor, such as the Archbishop of York. They have secured public participation, raised the profile of inequality in their area and produced analyses of inequality's nature and extent. Studies of the fairness commission movement have been produced by Carnegie UK,[50] the Local Government Innovation Unit,[51] the New Economics Foundation,[52] and the Webb Memorial

---

49 Newcastle Fairness Commission, *Fair share, fair play, fair go, fair say* (Newcastle: Newcastle City Council, 2012), www.ncl.ac.uk/media/wwwnclacuk/socialrenewal/files/fairnessreport.pdf, accessed 27 March 2017.
50 G. Irvine, *Fairness commissions from Shetland to Southampton* (Dunfermline: Carnegie UK Trust, 2017), www.carnegieuktrust.org.uk/carnegieuktrust/wp-content/uploads/sites/64/2017/06/Fairness-Commissions-from-Shetland-to-Southampton-the-role-of-Fairness-Commissions-in-the-Enabling-State.pdf, accessed 3 July 2017.
51 J. Sillett and C. O'Donnell, *Fairness commissions* (London: Local Government Information Unit, 2013), www.lgiu.org.uk/wp-content/uploads/2013/08/Fairness-Commissions.pdf, accessed 27 March 2017.
52 S. Lyall, *Fairness commissions: Understanding how local authorities can have an impact on inequality and poverty* (London: New Economics Foundation, 2015), http://b.3cdn.net/nefoundation/b9ee98970cb7f3065d_0hm6b0x2y.pdf, accessed 27 March 2017.

Trust with Edge Hill University.[53] Fairness commissions in the UK have convened on a number of occasions. International interest has been shown by the Friedrich Ebert Stiftung think-tank in Germany. I would be lying if I said running a fairness commission was all plain sailing. It was not. Sometimes we struggled to sustain partner organisations' engagement. The exercise relied heavily on committed individuals. I remain uncertain about the value of producing an interim report. We did not always synchronise the commission's schedule with our budget-setting timelines, meaning recommendations and resources were sometimes misaligned. We made one recommendation that it turned out, frustratingly, was not legally doable (namely, the outright banning of payday lenders). And, while we did right to focus on what we could do locally, we could also have made recommendations for regional and national government. Perhaps this is part of the reason, alongside any partisan qualms, the commission did not attract much central government interest from Westminster or Whitehall. Notwithstanding these mistakes and limitations, in Islington the fairness commission was a highly effective and influential piece of work. Might your area benefit from a similar approach?

Regardless of the model of change we adopt, sometimes progress will be slow. I find it helpful to keep in mind this chant: "What do we want? Gradual change! When do we want it? In due course!" There will also need to be compromises and pragmatism: there is a reason they say that politics is the art of the possible. We sometimes have to make trade-offs and prioritise. For instance, when we opened the first new Citizens Advice Bureau in London for 20 years in a high-profile location on Islington's Upper Street, we had to close our Green Living Centre to free up the space (though the Bureau does offer advice on, among other things, energy costs and fuel poverty). To make a real difference, we may well have to attend to detail that we would rather ignore: we may campaign in poetry but we tend to govern in prose. We may have to follow actions up time and again until they actually happen. But all of this is worth it, if it means we can get things done.

---

53 P. Bunyan and J. Diamond, *Approaches to reducing poverty and inequality in the UK: A study of civil society initiatives and fairness commissions* (Ormskirk: Edge Hill University, 2014), www.webbmemorialtrust.org.uk/download/publications_&_reports/CS-1452%20 Civil%20Society%2036pp%20A4%5b1%5d.pdf, accessed 27 March 2017.

CHAPTER 5

Equality in housing

We live in a rich country that is failing to house its people properly. Housing here is in chronic crisis. With house prices trebling in the decade before the 2008 financial crash, owning a home is out of reach for many without access to 'the Bank of Mum and Dad'. If we want to avoid inflating another major economic bubble, a return to self-certified, 100-per-cent loan-to-value, interest-only, and buy-to-let mortgages is not the answer. At the same time, government policy is marginalising social housing, which is fast becoming the preserve of only the poorest in society. Each homebuyer tends to be richer than the person from whom they buy. Each tenant who moves into a council flat tends to be poorer than their predecessor. These dynamics threaten to segregate our society, with communities divided along housing tenure lines. Often, those on our estates and on our streets barely mix. And so the gap grows.

As a result, more and more people – including, increasingly, families with children – are being funnelled into a private rented sector that is all too often substandard, unaffordable and insecure. Assured shorthold tenancies offer little by way of notice or security. Over 40 per cent of the private rented sector does not meet the Decent Homes Standard, despite the government ploughing over £9 billion a year into it in the form of Local Housing Allowance. Private rented accommodation is where many of what Theresa May calls the 'just about managing' and what Ed Miliband called 'the squeezed middle' now reside.

Tackling inequality in housing would mean once again making social housing a mixed tenure, as opposed to the preserve of the disadvantaged. It would mean a better-regulated private rented sector, as some people will always want the flexibility private renting brings. And it would mean making owner occupation more accessible to ordinary families. There is, after all, both a democratic argument for increasing home ownership – poll after poll tells us that British people want to own their own home – and a social argument too: people who own their own home enjoy a stability that lends itself to them getting involved in their local community. None of these developments is likely unless nationwide housebuilding can be dramatically increased. Even if a million new homes were built during this Parliament, which itself would be no mean feat, that would be enough merely to slow but not to stop the widening of the gap between supply and demand.[54]

Fixing the problem of housing supply is largely a question of finance. At the moment, 95 per cent of the country's housing expenditure is spent on Housing Benefit and only 5 per cent is spent on building new homes. It has not always been this way, and it must not continue as it is. In the late 1970s, 80 per cent of housing spend was on bricks and mortar. We have to shift back from subsidising rents to building homes, from benefits to bricks. In doing so, we must avoid repeating the mistakes of the 1980s, when private finance was introduced into social housing with a ghettoising effect, reducing space standards, increasing rents and denuding housing associations over time of their social purpose. To move forwards, we may need to decentralise. The case for doing so is strong. There is already huge local and regional variation in housing markets. What that means is that a one-size-fits-all approach run from Whitehall cannot work. We have to stop seeking a national welfare solution to a local housing problem. By devolving all housing spend to the local level – that is, both capital spend and Housing Benefit allocation – in a single 'affordable housing grant', local authorities could help us realise the benefits of bricks. At the moment, though, councils have no incentive to care about the level of Housing Benefit spending in their area because it does not come out of their pockets. This move would better align those incentives, even if the overall financial envelope remained the same. There are a number of ways that local authorities could use their affordable housing grants, depending on local circumstances, such as:

- doing long-term deals with private developers and housing associations to build new affordable homes for people to rent or buy
- establishing a local scheme to provide support for people on low incomes with their housing costs (as an alternative to national Housing Benefit)
- entering into agreements with private landlords to secure a better deal for tenants and taxpayers

54 K. Schmuecker, *The good, the bad and the ugly: Housing demand 2025* (London: Institute for Public Policy Research, 2011), www.ippr.org/publications/the-good-the-bad-and-the-ugly-housing-demand-2025, accessed 27 March 2017.

- purchasing existing properties not currently in residential use and bringing empty properties back into the market
- providing support to get people into employment and reduce worklessness, so that people are better able to meet their own housing costs.

Some of these options have been explored in Islington. The council, together with other London boroughs, does try to strike a collective deal to limit the cost of private rental flats for those in temporary accommodation. It also invests £3 million a year in employment-support initiatives, such as its iWork job coaches.

In these ways, local authorities could, over time, help us to effect a gradual shift back towards a better balance in the way our country spends its housing money.

Devolution aside, if the government were to lift the borrowing cap imposed on councils (which prevents them from building more council homes) rather than coming up with ever more gimmicks for prospective homebuyers, then we might be able to get somewhere.[55] These centrally imposed borrowing restrictions, which prevent local authorities from leveraging their assets and income, make us Europe's odd one out. We ought to be dropping fiscal policies centred on the public sector's borrowing requirement and replacing them with fiscal rules and accounting practices based on general government borrowing and debt, as used elsewhere in Europe. Public housing expenditure is, after all, an investment, not a sunken cost.

Institutional investment ought also to be possible to get new homes built. With collective investment vehicles forming all across the country, local-authority pension funds (worth over £150 billion nationally) are well placed now to invest in new build, as Greater Manchester Pension Fund has. Islington Pension Fund invests £20 million in residential property through its Hearthstone fund, mostly in privately rented properties predominantly in London and the South East. There need be no conflict with trustees' fiduciary duties.

To get more homes built, we also need to reform the mainstream

---

55 H. Richardson, 'Housing: Councils call for freedoms to build new homes', *BBC News*, 22 October 2016, www.bbc.co.uk/news/education-37729027, accessed 27 March 2017.

planning system. Too much low-value agricultural land and land that has previously been developed is classified as low-grade greenbelt. Councils need to create joined-up plans for increasing housing supply, working with neighbouring local authorities. We need more local lettings policies (like the one in Islington) that give existing residents more of a reason to support new development in their midst: if the downsides appear concrete and the upsides are only ever abstract, consent will always be difficult to achieve.

We are at our best when we are at our boldest, so I would want to see two further, more radical developments. The first would be the government levying a land value tax on undeveloped developable land above a certain threshold in value to encourage new building and raise funds for housing investment.[56] The second would be the establishment of a parallel strategic planning system to deliver a wave of new towns (though this is not to denigrate the importance of infill and densification).[57] 'New towns' programmes in the past have seen the highest level of new housebuilding in this country since World War II. Notwithstanding the formidable political obstacles and economic constraints such a policy would now face, we need to reform and revitalise this proven approach, rendering it fit for today's political and economic landscape. In doing so, we must avoid the social dysfunctionality observed in some previous new towns, which were born out of large-scale displacement to make room for slum clearance.

We need to shake up the development industry, which has had it too easy and too cosy for too long. The state gives big developers land, money and guarantees and gets too little by way of genuinely affordable housing in return. We should allow failing developers to go to the wall, with government then acting as a clearing house for their land banks. We should insist on rapid build-out and lower profit margins through public land programmes. And we should encourage local councils and the Mayor of London to release more public land for housebuilding in return for equity stakes that secure public benefit.

---

56 A. Hull, *In land revenue: The case for a land value tax in the UK* (London: Centre for Labour and Social Studies, 2013), http://labourlist.org/2013/05/in-land-revenue-the-case-for-a-land-value-tax-in-the-uk, accessed 27 March 2017.

57 G. Cooke and A. Hull, *Together at home: A new strategy for housing* (London: Institute for Public Policy Research, 2012), www.ippr.org/publications/together-at-home-a-new-strategy-for-housing, accessed 27 March 2017.

It is also important that housing be developed to cater for the full range of needs in our society. In particular, the needs of older residents could be better met.

New Earswick for All Ages

In researching the subject of housing, I had the pleasure of meeting with the Joseph Rowntree Foundation and the Joseph Rowntree Housing Trust (JRHT) in York, where there are 10,000 people on the council's housing waiting list. The JRHT's main mission is to tackle housing inequality. It invests in the community (using a social investment fund worth £10 million) according to Joseph Rowntree's vision of social investment to prevent social evils. Its approach is infused with its eponymous founder's Quaker philosophy, with its long-term perspective, mature attitude towards risk and deep engagement with the community. The JRHT has developed a project called New Earswick for All Ages, which has seen significant investment in a community for people at various stages of their lives.[58] The aim is for its housing to be accessible and attractive and to be offered alongside care services fit for an ageing society, enabling residents to 'age in place'. It has established an intergenerationally integrated lifelong neighbourhood, not one separated or segregated by age. Existing community assets, both physical and human, are optimised. Health and social care are joined up. Combating loneliness and supporting dementia are critical to the initiative. Carers are supported by being paid the (real) Living Wage, calculated based on the cost of living, which is a rarity in a residential adult social care setting.[59] New Earswick for All Ages could not be further from the decrepit and dilapidated state of too much of the country's adult social care provision after years of inadequate funding and political neglect.

We also need to use our existing housing stock better. For a start, that has to mean leaving less of it sitting empty.

---

58 See Joseph Rowntree Housing Trust, www.jrht.org.uk/community/new-earswick-york, accessed 27 March 2017.
59 By 'real' living wage, I mean the voluntary hourly rate administered by the independent Living Wage Foundation, based upon the actual cost of living, as opposed to the government's lower, statutory so-called National Living Wage, which applies only to those aged 25 or over.

Abolish Empty Office Buildings

Last year, again as part of my research, I met a gentleman called Tony Crofts. Tony is a Quaker who joined the Friends in Oxford in the 1970s. Today, he is the founder and director of Abolish Empty Office Buildings (AEOB) in Bristol, where he is in the business of 'recycling spaces'.[60] AEOB has teamed up with Triodos Bank and harnesses ethical investment via community shares to buy wasteful, empty commercial properties and convert them into affordable homes, cooperatively run, for people who need them. Fellow Quakers have provided the training for tenants to run the co-op. In Bristol alone, where people need an income of £70,000 to buy a flat on the open market and where the social housing waiting list is 14,000 people long, there are apparently 2.2 million square feet of unused office space. At the end of 2016, AEOB unveiled its first six units of social housing in what had been disused commercial premises.[61] What I heard in Bristol was an excellent example of the power to be found not only in organised people but also in organised money.

We should be using incentives to get the owners of empty or underoccupied homes to bring them into full residential use. Such incentives could include removing the council tax discount on long-term empty properties, encouraging local authorities to use empty dwelling management orders more often, and uprating the relief on income tax on renting out a spare room in line with the Retail Price Index.

We also need to support the development of new homeshare schemes.[62] This is something many of us can do in our local community. Take, for example, the Fair BnB pilot developed by the Campaign Company off the back of the Croydon Opportunity & Fairness Commission.[63] Its aim is to prevent homelessness before it occurs by matching hosts with spare rooms to families who have

---

60 See *Abolish Empty Office Buildings*, www.aeobhousepeople.org.uk, accessed 27 March 2017.

61 See information on AEOB's formal launch in December 2016 at 'Formal Launch', *Abolish Empty Office Buildings*, 17 December 2016, www.aeobhousepeople.org.uk/posts/2016/12, accessed 27 March 2017.

62 S. Butler, 'Homeshare: Meet the unlikely housemates', *The Guardian*, 16 March 2012, www.theguardian.com/lifeandstyle/2012/mar/16/homeshare-unlikely-housemates, accessed 27 March 2017.

63 See *Fairbnb*, www.fairbnb.org.uk/about, accessed 27 March 2017.

fallen on hard times and need a roof over their heads. These kinds of schemes usually involve a paid coordinator screening and then matching, for instance, an older person who owns their home and has a spare room to offer with a young person who then becomes in effect their lodger. Both parties agree to a code of conduct and sometimes pay a small fee to fund the coordination and administrative support. Often the lodger undertakes to provide a certain number of hours each week of help to the host, for example with cooking, shopping or cleaning.

Such schemes can be 'win–wins', addressing a manifest need while promoting intergenerational interaction. They can help to tackle social isolation among older people, providing support that allows them to remain living independently in the community, even reducing the costs to the NHS – for instance, as a result of falls. But they also enable young people of limited means to access secure, decent and affordable accommodation.

Lack of supply is not the only driver of inequality in housing, though. More robust regulation to strike a better deal for those who rent privately would also help. Private landlords could be required to sign up to a national register, just as registered social landlords are. Landlord licensing schemes should be made mandatory. Longer tenancies, for instance, with a five-year secure period and a five-month notice period, could be developed. In addition, rent stabilisation could be introduced in hotspots (as it has been in New York) to cap rent rises rather than absolute values. Legislation that currently allows minimal furnishing of a home to class it as occupied for tax-avoidance purposes could also be tightened to address the 'buy-to-leave' phenomenon prevalent in places such as Islington.

If we did all of this, then reform and resources would enable housing supply to meet demand; home ownership would become more affordable to more people; social housing would become more mixed and mainstreamed; private renting would be better quality and more secure; more people could enjoy a stable, decent, ample, and affordable home; and housing could be a force for integration – and equality – in our society.

CHAPTER 6

Equality at work

If the housing market can compound inequality in the UK, the job market can drive it. But it would be a mistake to try to divide the population of the UK crudely into 'skivers' and 'strivers'. As John Hills argues in his book *Good times, bad times: The welfare myth of them and us,* such a simplistic dichotomy is inaccurate and unhelpful.[64] At various stages in our lives, and whether we realise it or not, we all benefit from the welfare state and the social security it affords us. There is no doubt, however, that if we are to unlock the most pressing socio-economic problems in many of our communities, then employment is the key.

The failure, then, of the Department for Work and Pensions, through Jobcentre Plus and Work Programme providers, to support hard-to-reach job-seekers in finding sustained employment is a national blight. But, without the resources to rise to the challenge, hard-pressed local authorities will not be able to intervene in the job market to put right what the government has got so wrong. If government were to devolve the power, money and responsibility for supporting those furthest from the job market to local authorities, together with funding for crucial skills work, then councils would be well placed to play a valuable role in getting their communities back to work.

Many readers will work in organisations that can make a contribution in this area by providing employment opportunities for local people. This could include forging links with local schools, offering careers advice, coaching, mentoring, and work experience. A summer placement can make all the difference in someone picking up basic skills, such as punctuality and persistence, that are necessary to get on in the world of work. Businesses can offer apprenticeships, paid internships and traineeships. Employers can practise anonymous shortlisting in recruitment to avoid inadvertent discrimination. They can ensure their premises are fully accessible for disabled people. They can offer flexible, job-shared and part-time work to fit in with people's caring responsibilities and support for childcare, such as childcare loans. They can ensure employee representation on their remuneration board and recognise trade

---

64 J. Hills, *Good times, bad times: The welfare myth of them and us* (Bristol: Policy Press, 2014).

unions. And they can insist that throughout their supply chain their suppliers do some of this as well. The Islington Fairness Commission recommended all of this (see Annex A for details of its implementation). Does the organisation where you work do some or all of it? Could you help it to?

Getting a job is important, but in-work poverty also remains a shameful feature of Britain today. An irresponsible form of capitalism, typified by the privatisation of profit and the socialisation of loss, has led us on a wages race to the bottom. Companies have got away with it because they have been propped up by 'corporate welfare'. So, big retailers currently pay many of their shop-floor staff poverty wages, safe in the knowledge that, through mechanisms such as tax credits and Housing Benefit, the government will effectively bail these firms out. Their bosses may contend that if they paid their staff properly then that would hit the firms' profitability, but, with companies having operating profits measured in millions of pounds a year, I would have little sympathy for any such retort. A prerequisite of any sustainable industrial strategy must be a resolute rejection of poverty pay.

Every fairness commission held so far has identified income inequality as a major challenge, and most have recommended, as a measure to address it, local implementation of the annually uprated (real) Living Wage (at the time of writing, £9.40 per hour in London and £8.25 per hour elsewhere), which is independently calculated based on the actual cost of living.[65] There is a clear need for such action, given that more than one in five UK workers – over five million people – now earn less than the Living Wage.[66]

The Living Wage is about money, yes, but it is also about ideas. By this I mean that it is about living, not just surviving; that it is a wage, not a handout; and that it is about earning, contribution, reciprocity, and the dignity of work. When it is won not by someone in Whitehall pulling a lever but by workers themselves campaigning in the workplace, it can be about politics done with people, not just

65 See *Living Wage Foundation*, www.livingwage.org.uk, accessed 27 March 2017.
66 A. Corlett and L. Gardiner, *Low pay Britain 2015* (London: Resolution Foundation, 2015), www.resolutionfoundation.org/app/uploads/2015/10/Low-Pay-Britain-2015.pdf, accessed 27 March 2017.

for them. I have seen hardened chief executives, impervious to suits and their management-speak, melt when their cleaners narrate their lived experience to their face. That is the power of testimony and a true example of the sort of democratic (not only economic) levelling that I mentioned as important before.

The Living Wage is important for employees, employers and society as a whole. For employees, it means quitting that second job, getting some sleep, catching one Tube to work instead of two buses, buying Christmas presents this year, having a family holiday, and spending some time with the kids. For employers, it means higher staff morale, improved rates of retention, lower rates of sickness and absence, and reputational gain. And for society, it is important that no one should have to do a hard day's work for less than they can live on. By working, people ought to be able to earn their keep as well as enjoy some quality time with their friends and family.

Over the past decade, the Living Wage campaign, led by Citizens UK, has lifted over 45,000 families out of working poverty, putting more than £210 million of increased wages into the pockets of low-paid workers. Significant successes for the campaign have included the Greater London Authority, businesses in the City, hospitals, universities, and the Olympic and Paralympic Games London 2012. The next fronts include retail, hospitality and football. Perhaps you can help.

In Islington, urging local employers to pay their staff and contractors the Living Wage was the top recommendation of our fairness commission's final report in 2011. In 2012, Islington Council became the UK's first accredited Living Wage local authority, securing the Living Wage for all 5,000 of its own staff. In 2013, the council reviewed all its contracts and built a Living Wage requirement into its £500 million per annum procurement activity, securing the Living Wage for 92 per cent of its contractors. In 2014, this figure climbed to 98 per cent as the council won the Living Wage for all 519 of its home-care workers, including for their travel time between appointments. In 2015, Islington obtained the Living Wage for workers at one of its residential care homes, St Anne's, and became the first public-sector body to be accredited as a Living Wage Friendly Funder, building a Living Wage requirement into its core grant-giving to charities. The council's challenge remains the rest of its contracted residential social care workforce, who constitute the remaining 2 per cent of its contractors who still do not receive the Living Wage. Cracking this is far from easy. Adult social care is an industry in which the dominant business model is predicated on low pay, where overall costs are predominantly made up of staff wages, and where private providers operate minimal margins. When the contractors enjoy lengthy contracts and also own the care homes in question, renegotiating pay with them is extremely hard.

Islington Council throughout this time has also sought to offer civic leadership by exerting influence outside its immediate authority, convincing other employers in the borough to pay their staff the Living Wage as well. This approach has proved successful with employers across the public sector (e.g. Islington Clinical Commissioning Group, London Metropolitan University and over 15 schools), the voluntary sector (e.g. Amnesty International, Child Poverty Action Group and Save the Children), big businesses (e.g. Slaughter and May), and small firms (e.g. Casual Films). As a result, Islington is now the local authority area with the second highest number (110) of accredited Living Wage Employers in the UK. There is still more to do, though, with certain large local employers such as Arsenal FC still not paying (for instance) their legion of match-day caterers the Living Wage. Finally, Islington Council's £1 billion pension fund has engaged in shareholder activism, attending annual general meetings to lobby FTSE 100 companies such as Sainsbury's to pay the Living Wage, with some success.

Leading by example and tackling low pay in this way has not been easy for a council whose government funding is being cut by 70 per cent in the space of a decade. Committing to paying the Living Wage entails a degree of uncertainty, as it is uprated each year and the amount by which it rises is not predetermined. Embracing the Living Wage can affect an organisation's pay scales and make it more difficult to maintain differentials between grades at the bottom of its income distribution. But, truth be told, it does not have to break the bank.

Securing the Living Wage for contractors poses its own set of problems. But layers of contracting should not absolve employers of their responsibility for those who, in the end, work for them: out of sight must not mean out of mind. It is often possible to review contracts and renegotiate them assertively, where necessary. In my experience, it is always worth asking the question of contractors – could they possibly pay the Living Wage? – rather than assuming that the answer is no. There may be contracts too that straddle boundaries between organisations. In these cases, I would say it would be a mistake to let the perfect become the enemy of the good. If one organisation is up for leading the way and paying the Living Wage, while waiting for the other(s) to follow, then it can strike specific subsidiary Living Wage terms and conditions within the relevant consortium.

As for new procurement, this is where a paradigm shift is required. For decades, organisations across all sectors of the UK economy have sought to drive their costs down. In most cases, this has led to downward pressure on wages. Procurement staff have been asked for years to secure the lowest cost, so asking them to secure the Living Wage for contractors can appear paradoxical, at first. There are legal hurdles to surmount as well, not least negotiating the European Union's Posted Workers Directive, but varied precedents show this is perfectly possible. Unions can then be enlisted to help ensure contractors do not employ any clever workarounds to try to avoid paying their staff properly. Finally, it is worth being aware in advance that detailed Living Wage questions can get a bit messy when it comes to the likes of apprentices, interns and work experience. In the end, though, everyone who cooks school meals, staffs gyms and swimming pools, and keeps offices safe and clean deserves to earn enough to live on in return for a hard day's work.

Over 1,700 organisations nationally are now accredited as Living Wage Employers, including 45 local authorities. When local government secures the Living Wage through procurement, this lessens the strain on the welfare state, effectively shifting more of the burden to the private sector from the public purse. Indeed, to catalyse this process, the government could agree to share with local authorities the benefits to the exchequer of councils getting their contractors to adopt the Living Wage. Central government could also do more to drive a Living Wage requirement through its own procurement processes, as many local authorities have. Moreover, government should incentivise businesses to adopt the Living Wage, as proposed by Ed Miliband in the run-up to the 2015 general election, giving a time-limited tax rebate to private companies that raise the wages of their lowest-paid staff.[67]

Quaker Living Wage Campaign

Quakers are already doing some excellent work on fairer pay. I visited Ann Morgan in Lancaster to hear about her work on the Living Wage.[68] She had attended a session titled 'Food Banks Are Not Enough' at a Quaker conference in October 2014, put on by Central England Quakers. Afterwards, Ann felt moved to do something about what she had heard. She started a small local group to campaign on the Living Wage and met with her local MP, Cat Smith. The local meeting agreed to run a stall at Christmas 2014 in Lancaster and three people agreed to help. Their campaign grew ahead of the general election in 2015 and developed into a local Quaker Equality Week. Ann and her crew have since gone on to lead a national Quaker Living Wage Campaign,[69] with a committee of six. They devised a support pack for other meetings. In the pack, there are suggestions as to what groups can do, such as pushing local authorities and universities to become accredited as Living Wage Employers, lobbying the directors of the Co-operative Group or mounting a vigil during the Edinburgh Festival. The theme of Yearly Meeting Gathering 2017 is 'movement-building': people like Ann are doing just that.

York Area Quaker Meeting is now accredited as a Living Wage Employer. Other meetings are applying now. It is a slow but thorough process that has thrown up some interesting questions, including around employment law, for instance regarding wardens' modes of remuneration. Britain Yearly Meeting and Friends House Hospitality Limited in Euston are both accredited Living Wage Employers, as are Quaker Social Action, Quaker Service in Northern Ireland and Quaker area meetings in Lancashire Central & North, Manchester & Warrington,

67 BBC, 'Ed Miliband pledges living wage tax breaks for firms', *BBC News*, 3 November 2013, www.bbc.co.uk/news/uk-24786397, accessed 27 March 2017.
68 See 'A Quaker Living Wage Campaign', *Lancashire Quakers*, www.lancsquakers.org.uk/livingwagecampaign.php, accessed 27 March 2017.
69 See 'Living Wage', *Quakers in Britain*, www.quaker.org.uk/our-work/economic-justice/living-wage, accessed 27 March 2017.

and Mid-Thames. Bootham School in York, which maintains the Quaker ethos, pays the Living Wage but does not increase its pay each year until September (as opposed to April), and so is not a fully accredited Living Wage Employer yet. Woodbrooke Quaker Study Centre does pay the Living Wage and at the time of writing is working towards accreditation. Other Quaker centres, such as Claridge House and Glenthorne, are investigating the possibility of becoming Living Wage Employers. There are sample Living Wage letters on the website so that Friends can write to employers to urge them to do the right thing.

I was impressed by this example of civil society forging a fairer society itself, rather than looking to statutory authorities to do so. It was also a useful reminder for me that Quakers themselves are, of course, employers and businesspeople and can make a real difference in such capacities in their places of work.

The voluntary (real) Living Wage is important, but there remain too many workers (conservatively estimated at 300,000[70]) in the UK who put in shifts for less than the statutory National Minimum Wage. There is a good argument for the Department for Business, Energy & Industrial Strategy to devolve responsibility for enforcing compliance with the National Minimum Wage to local authorities. The existing, overly centralised institutional architecture for National Minimum Wage enforcement is not fit for purpose. HM Revenue & Customs is too distant from communities to deal effectively with the many sharp practices that occur at the local level. Closer to the ground, local authorities have existing, multifaceted relationships with employers and with workers in their area. Combined with councils keeping newly increased fines for non-compliance, such a localised arrangement could be self-financing.

Finally, on income inequality and pay, the government should require all employers to publish their internal pay ratios between their highest-paid and lowest-paid (as opposed to average-paid) employees, bringing much-needed transparency to the low-pay-versus-high-pay debate. The political economist Will Hutton has suggested that,

70 A. Hull, *Settle for nothing less: Enhancing national minimum wage compliance and enforcement* (London: Centre for London, 2013), www.centreforlondon.org/wp-content/uploads/2016/08/CFL-Settle-for-Nothing-Less.pdf, accessed 27 March 2017.

under normal circumstances, no public-sector employer should exhibit an internal pay ratio higher than 1:20.[71] Since introducing the real London Living Wage at the bottom of the pay scale while cutting the salary of the chief executive at the top, Islington Council now has a pay ratio of 1:9. For context, in the Co-operative Group (as an example), the pay ratio stands at 1:47. The ratio at Friends House in London is narrow at 1:4. That of Britain Yearly Meeting as a whole is 1:5. At Woodbrooke Quaker Study Centre, it is 1:3. The Islington Fairness Commission recommended major local employers should all publish their pay ratios, in the hope that transparency will bring scrutiny and, in time, progress. If the gap matters, as I believe it does, we have to challenge the idea that dramatic pay inequality is alright and that pay restraint is unnecessary at the top.

71 BBC, 'Best-to-worst public sector pay link proposed by Hutton', *BBC News*, 1 December 2010, www.bbc.co.uk/news/business-11879059, accessed 27 March 2017.

CHAPTER 7

Equality in other fields
of public policy

Dealing with debt

Inequality in people's income can be compounded by the debts they owe. Nevertheless, it would be a mistake to assume that problem debt only affects those at the bottom of the income distribution. Some high earners are deeply indebted, although they may be better placed to service that debt. Quaker Social Action does some excellent work to help low-income households struggling to manage their finances.[72] For example, the Down to Earth project supports disadvantaged families to finance proper funerals for their loved ones.

Through the Islington Fairness Commission (and others around the country, most of which were held in deprived areas), we have heard how widespread problem debt is in inner-city areas, where rich and poor are often juxtaposed, cheek by jowl. High-quality advice for those who find themselves in such a predicament is critical. Recognising this, and heeding the commission's recommendations, Islington Council opened the first new Citizens Advice Bureau in London for 20 years, in a high-profile high-street location. It is now dealing with over a thousand clients each month. The Bureau then launched the Fit Money project, to do financial literacy work with social tenants in the borough. In my view, this subject merits greater attention in the PSHE (personal, social, health, and economic education) curricula of our secondary schools. Alongside this preventative work, Islington Council sought to secure enforcement against pernicious payday lenders – 'legal loan sharks' – who were not playing by the industry's (already light-touch) rules; councillors were at the forefront of the national Sharkstoppers campaign. Together with my fellow North London MP Stella Creasy and the community organisers of the sadly now-defunct Movement for Change, they campaigned successfully for the Financial Conduct Authority to impose a national cap on the cost of credit, meaning borrowers should never have to pay back more than twice what they borrowed overall. Together with advice on how to avoid or escape debt and enforcement against unscrupulous lenders, the council

---

72 See 'Quaker Social Action', *Quakers in the World*, www.quakersintheworld.org/quakers-in-action/346, accessed 27 March 2017.

also promoted a socially just alternative in the form of London Capital Credit Union (LCCU). A large proportion of the council's staff and members now save regularly with LCCU through a payroll deduction scheme. Other employers could be lobbied to offer such a scheme. For example, if the NHS did, it would make it easier for 1.5 million workers to access affordable credit.

Government does not make it as easy as it could for place-shaping local authorities to prevent the proliferation of undesirable high-cost credit stores or betting shops, with their dangerously addictive fixed-odds betting terminals. National planning law currently makes it difficult for councils' planning committees to stop such outfits from opening on their high streets if such applications do not necessitate a change of use class for the premises in question. If a bank closes a branch, it is too easy for a payday lender to open in its place. For these reasons, Islington Council was able to honour the spirit but not the letter of the fairness commission's recommendation that it pass a by-law to ban payday lenders locally outright. Government could and should introduce a specific use class for such organisations, empowering planning authorities to limit their spread.

Equal from the start

The most divisive inequalities are those that are evident from an early age. This is why tackling child poverty must remain high on the national political agenda and it is why the Islington Fairness Commission put a heavy emphasis on the need to prioritise measures that would help to address inequality in childhood. As a result, the council focused efforts on early years, school and college interventions.

Many of the fairness commissions to date have identified a lack of accessible, affordable childcare as an issue. In Islington, the First 21 Months project was recommended by the commission and then established with local health partners to ensure coordinated support was available for every child during gestation and throughout the first year of life. Such help ranged from peer support commissioned from the voluntary sector for mothers struggling with breastfeeding through enhanced health visiting for troubled families and intensive intervention from family support workers. When Sure Start children's centres were closing in most parts of the country, Islington kept all of its open, despite relentless government cuts. A Childcare Coalition was formed – again a fairness commission recommendation – to make sure the childcare on offer across the borough met modern parents' needs: maximum flexibility, free childcare wherever possible, and a policy of keeping any unavoidable costs low and unhidden.

Islington introduced free school meals for all primary school children up to Year 6 (age 11) to address both health-orientated and educational concerns. This has reduced stigmatising division between classmates and meant that each child has a hot, nutritious meal each day, enabling them to concentrate in order to learn better and preventing them from overdosing on sugar and disrupting the learning of their peers. It has also meant all kids are learning to eat with a knife and fork and to speak to adults at mealtimes, while saving hard-working families some much-needed cash. If the government were to roll this policy out nationally for all children up to the age of 11, it would be £400 million well spent.

The Islington Fairness Commission also flagged up the challenges the borough faces when it comes to levels of literacy. To address these, the commission recommended and the council then mounted a major drive called Islington Reads,[73] which seeks to raise aspiration and achievement in children and young people through the promotion of reading. Its annual elements include a Summer Reading Challenge in primary schools and an annual Archway with Words festival, which offers a host of activities for children and adults, from phonetics to performance poetry, in one of the borough's more deprived areas.

Our prioritisation of young people in Islington also led to the creation in 2011 of the Islington Youth Council.[74] The youth councillors, elected by their peers in schools throughout the borough, come from a wide array of backgrounds – by their own admission,

---

73 See 'Islington reads', *Islington Council*, www.islington.gov.uk/libraries-arts-and-heritage/ libraries/reading-learning-and-outreach-services/read-with-us/islington-reads, accessed 27 March 2017.

74 See 'More about your Youth Council', *Islington Council*, http://directory.islington.gov.uk/ kb5/islington/directory/youth.page?youthchannelnew=5_1, accessed 27 March 2017.

they are not all 'goody two-shoes' – and help to inform decisions made at the council about the services young people use. They take co-production seriously and the council's services end up better for it.

We also decided to part-replace the Education Maintenance Allowance of up to £30 a week for students in further education, which the government had cut. We thought it was important to enable young people to afford to go to college. Budgets were tight at the council – they are even tighter now, with the borough losing over 70 per cent of its core government funding in a decade since 2010 – but we had to put our money where our mouth was if we wanted to make further education in Islington accessible to all. Where possible, the council has sought to fund such measures through new income-generation activity (e.g. selling pest-control services to private citizens), asset optimisation (e.g. sharing buildings with other public-sector bodies), channel shift (to online transactions rather than telephone interactions), and shared services (e.g. sharing digital services with the neighbouring boroughs of Camden and Haringey).

Equally safe and secure

Inequality leads some to want what others have and so is a significant driver of acquisitive crime. A precursor to criminal behaviour is often behaviour that is antisocial. As an authority committed to early intervention, Islington Council responded positively to the fairness commission's recommendation that a single antisocial behaviour hotline be established, underpinned by a better-coordinated back-office, rather than relying on multiple housing providers to each have their own separate numbers. That hotline now receives over a thousand calls a month, with a consistent response coordinated across the council, police and housing associations. Given antisocial behaviour can also be a precursor to more serious crime, it is important to intervene early through targeted work with people and places to prevent problems from escalating. The council has also invested £2 million in upgrading closed-circuit television throughout the borough.

Another pernicious area of criminal activity is hate crime, which saw a nationwide spike following the EU referendum. Everyone deserves equal protection from discriminatory treatment, and harassment and victimisation should not have to be normalised the way they sadly often are. Hijabi women should not have to expect to get spat at or called names on the street. It is an area where we do need victims and witnesses to report more, and with more specificity – for instance, reporting relevant vehicles' registration numbers and descriptions of suspects' clothing, including through reporting schemes run by national and local charities. But it is also an area where we need the police to catch more of the culprits and sanction them accordingly. When they do, the police ought to publicise these successes to build community confidence in reporting.

Nothing endangers a family's security as much as war. Just watching the footage from Aleppo in late 2016, for instance, was a harrowing experience. I want the UK to be a country that offers safe passage and refuge for those fleeing the perils of war. It is important that we play our part in taking in Syrian refugees fleeing the carnage in their country. Citizens UK has done some sterling work to identify appropriate accommodation for such refugees and convince landlords to take a hit on their rent in order to take refugees in. Haringey has to its credit taken in ten Syrian refugee families. And the Big Green Bookshop in Wood Green collected from residents and then took much-needed supplies to the 'Jungle' camp in Calais before it was closed. I have been proud too of the reaction of British Quakers to the refugee crisis we have watched unfold.[75] Equality is meaningless without security and too many people in our world today feel insecure.

75 See 'Refugees', *Quakers in Britain*, www.quaker.org.uk/about-quakers/inspired-by-faith/refugees, accessed 27 March 2017.

CHAPTER 8

Equality as both end and means

Through this book, I have sought to give expression to Quaker testimony to equality as a central tenet of our faith. I have reflected upon the current state of dramatic inequality in the UK and the world today. Having diagnosed the problem, I have tried to show that we can all in our own way be a part of the solution. I have argued that democratic politics – both participatory and representative – is the best mechanism available to us to secure the change we want to see. However, I have cautioned too that, when making the case for greater equality, we need to use language and frames to which everybody can relate. This almost certainly means fewer big-picture graphs and more real-life stories.

Next, I have made the case that we can each do our bit to bring about a more equal world, starting with striving for fairness on the ground, where it counts. Then, I have dealt in turn with five of the areas of inequality that seem to me to be priorities for us to tackle – a view corroborated by the 32 fairness commissions the UK has seen so far. Firstly, there is the growing problem of inequality in the housing market, with rising prices, insufficient housebuilding and a burgeoning private rented sector that is under-regulated. Secondly, there is inequality in the world of work, in particular when it comes to fair remuneration. Thirdly, problem debt, now commonplace in many of our communities, is exacerbated by irresponsible lenders. Fourthly, those inequalities that set in during childhood and adolescence must be tackled. And fifthly, we have seen how unequal things can be when it comes to safety, security and the rule of law. In each of these five areas, I have gone on to suggest ways in which individuals, communities, the authorities, and local, regional and national government can act to make a difference.

All of this matters, for me, not just because economic equality is important as an end in itself, although that is undoubtedly true, but also because it is a critical means. It is a means to a healthier society,[76] characterised by greater respect and less anxiety. More equal societies are not just more productive; they are happier, have lower levels of depression and suicide, show fewer signs of status

---

76 Marmot Review, *Fair society, healthy lives* (London: Marmot Review, 2010), www. instituteofhealthequity.org/Content/FileManager/pdf/fairsocietyhealthylives.pdf, accessed 27 March 2017.

competition, and exhibit more peaceful psychology. A world that is more equal economically would be a world that is spiritually better balanced as well.

I believe we can help to bring such a world about. Quakers over the centuries have acted on this same conviction. I hope that, after reading this book, it will speak to your condition and that you will feel empowered and inspired to do so too.

Annex A: Recommendations of the Islington Fairness Commission and updates on their implementation

INCOME

RECOMMENDATION 1: WAGES
No one in Islington should do a hard day's work for less than they can live on.

Employers in Islington should pay all their directly employed staff as a minimum the London Living Wage (set at £8.30/hour back in 2011). Employers should also review their procurement, contract and best-value policies to ensure that, as far as possible within UK and EU law, the London Living Wage is the minimum paid to all their contracted staff as well.

Implementation: Islington Council became the first accredited Living Wage local authority in the UK. It now pays at least the real London Living Wage to 100 per cent of its staff and 98 per cent of its contractors. It has built a Living Wage stipulation into its procurement policy for its £500 million per annum of contracts. It requires its voluntary-sector grant recipients to pay at least the London Living Wage as well. As a result of its civic leadership, there are now at least 110 other accredited Living Wage Employers in Islington – one of the highest concentrations in the country. The council's pension fund is an active shareholder in various FTSE 100 firms and has lobbied those firms in which it invests to adopt the Living Wage, with some success.

RECOMMENDATION 2: PAY DIFFERENTIALS
Tackling income inequality is crucial to forging a fairer Islington.

All major employers in the borough should publish their pay differentials to enable them to be scrutinised and challenged where appropriate. In the case of Islington Council, this should mean establishing a formal subcommittee, including officer, member and union representation, to review pay differentials within the organisation with a view to reducing income inequality where possible.

Implementation: Islington Council cut its chief executive's pay by £50,000 and introduced the London Living Wage as a minimum salary for all its staff. As a result, the internal pay ratio at the council is now down to 1:9 (lowest paid:highest paid). The council has also signed up to the Pay Compare transparency scheme for pay differentials. The council has not made progress in terms of getting other employers in the borough to publish their pay differentials, as it has focused instead on successfully championing the Living Wage with employers throughout Islington.

RECOMMENDATION 3: DEBT

Personal debt compounds poverty and inequality, and may worsen as people in Islington lose their jobs.

Islington Council should explore the possibility of passing a by-law to prevent payday-loan companies from operating in the borough. And it should vigorously use its enforcement powers and those of its partners to take action against illegal activity by loan sharks who prey on vulnerable Islington residents.

Implementation: Islington Council has developed a three-pronged strategy for dealing with problem debt caused by payday lenders. First, it opened the first new Citizens Advice Bureau in London for 20 years and then helped the Bureau secure a £1 million grant from the Big Lottery Fund to establish Fit Money, a financial literacy project doing preventative work with young people on Islington council estates. Second, while a new by-law proved impossible, the council did take enforcement action via Trading Standards against payday lenders in the borough not abiding by relevant law and regulation and it did play a leading role in the national Sharkstoppers campaign, which successfully secured a national cap on the cost of credit from the then chancellor, cutting the payday lending industry in half. Third, the council has bolstered an alternative to payday lenders in the form of support for London Capital Credit Union (LCCU), one of the fastest growing credit unions in the country, not least through signing up hundreds of council members and staff to membership of LCCU in the form of payroll deduction.

WORK

RECOMMENDATION 4: EMPLOYMENT
Employment for Islington's residents is the best way to tackle poverty in the borough.

Employers in Islington should, by means of legitimate positive action (such as advertising job opportunities in local media before national media), increase the proportion of local people they employ, especially among currently under-represented groups, such as disabled people. In the case of Islington Council, this should mean increasing the proportion of Islington residents in its workforce from 23 per cent to 30 per cent by 2014.

Implementation: Islington Council has an extensive and successful programme of employment-support work, costing £3 million in 2017/18 and helping 2,700 Islington residents secure work since 2014. In 2012, 27.5 per cent of the council's employees were Islington residents.

RECOMMENDATION 5: JOBS FOR YOUNG PEOPLE
No young person in Islington should be altogether out of education, employment and training.

Employers in Islington should do more to support young people who are at risk of falling into the cycle of poverty. In particular, they should support the new initiatives being developed to this end by Islington Business Board, including its programme of mentoring and work experience, which will support young people in gaining employment or training or help them to start a business of their own.

Implementation: The council part-replaced the Education Maintenance Allowance, which had been cut by the government. The council's Youth Employment Strategy, including apprenticeships, work experience and mentoring, helped to halve unemployment among those aged 18–24 in the borough by 2015. The council has also introduced an elected Youth Council to represent and champion the views of young people in every area of the council's business.

RECOMMENDATION 6: CORPORATE SOCIAL RESPONSIBILITY

We need businesses and charities in Islington to be on the side of fairness.

Islington Chamber of Commerce and its partners should develop a plan to promote the following important activities among businesses and charities in the borough, for example through a Fair Islington kitemark scheme:

- pay at least the London Living Wage to all staff
- have a pay differential of less than 1:20
- ensure access to both premises and opportunities for disabled people
- offer apprenticeships and/or paid internships
- offer work-experience placements
- have employee representation on remuneration panels
- recognise trade unions
- offer family-friendly employment practices, including flexible and part-time working and job-sharing opportunities
- offer support for childcare, including childcare loans
- support workless people to prepare for the world of employment.

Implementation: Islington Council decided, in consultation with business representatives, to focus its 'asks' of local businesses in just two areas: paying the Living Wage (see above) and hiring apprentices locally (facilitated by the council's Business Employment Support Team). Meanwhile, the council itself has become an accredited Timewise employer (for offering flexible employment), has signed the Ethical Care Charter regarding its approach to domiciliary care staff (which concerns, for example, paid travel time and eliminating visits lasting under 15 minutes), and has signed the Dying to Work pledge, signifying a commitment to support terminally ill staff.

FAMILIES

RECOMMENDATION 7: THE FIRST YEAR, AND BEFORE

What happens during pregnancy and a child's first year is crucial to a child's life chances.

There should be a major review, convened by the new Health and Wellbeing Board, of all public-, private- and voluntary-sector activity in Islington to support parents and parents-to-be from the point of a child's conception to his or her first birthday. In particular, this review should look at significantly improving the coordination of services, especially those delivered by GPs, midwives, health visitors, and the council.

Implementation: The council coordinated the multi-agency First 21 Months project, specifically improving children's centres' links with GPs and their reach into disadvantaged communities. Antenatal maternity care in the community has also been stepped up.

RECOMMENDATION 8: AFFORDABLE CHILDCARE
A lack of affordable childcare is a serious barrier to parents returning to work.

Islington Council and its partners should establish a local Childcare Coalition, involving schools, public-sector organisations, the voluntary sector (e.g. Islington Childcare Trust), and employers to increase the amount of affordable childcare available in the borough, especially during school holidays. This should include, for example, protecting after-school clubs, despite cuts to their public funding. The Childcare Coalition should also work to persuade employers to support parents in working flexibly around childcare provision.

Implementation: Islington Council protected all the borough's children's centres and established both a Childcare Coalition and a Parental Employment Partnership. The council also persuaded the Co-op and Waitrose locally to offer more flexible working arrangements to job-seeking parents in the borough.

RECOMMENDATION 9: ISLINGTON READS
The ability to read is essential for a fairer Islington.

A new community collaboration should be set up, organised by a partnership of public-sector and voluntary-sector organisations, to share reading skills across communities in Islington. This will help both children and adults to improve their literacy.

Implementation: The Islington Reads literacy drive was set up by Islington Council in 2012 and is still going today. Its features include the annual Word Festival, the Teen Reads Vote and the Summer Reading Challenge for schoolchildren. Other related initiatives include reading support in Pentonville Prison and coordinated donation of books for homeless people.

COMMUNITY

Recommendation 10: Giving time, giving money
Giving time and giving money is a good way of challenging poverty and inequality in our borough.
Islington Giving should be supported to:
- champion Islington's needs and encourage residents and businesses to donate time and money to the campaign
- continue its efforts to recruit, train and deploy 500 or more new volunteers in the borough by 2014
- establish a new Good Neighbours scheme to reduce social isolation, particularly among older and disabled people, and build community spirit in the borough.

Islington Council should, with Voluntary Action Islington, coordinate the valuable volunteering time it affords its employees, so that such efforts are targeted at Islington recipients in greatest need.
Implementation: Islington Giving (led by ancient local charity the Cripplegate Foundation) recruited over 500 new volunteers in the borough and raised in excess of £2 million following the Islington Fairness Commission. Cripplegate also piloted a Good Neighbours project to tackle social isolation on the New River Green Estate with 40 residents. Recently, the council has internally recruited a host of 'digital champions' to assist local residents with getting online.

Recommendation 11: Public space
We need to reclaim, protect and maintain communal spaces in Islington for community use.
Islington Council and partners should identify all unused communal

space in Islington, especially on estates, to free it up, make it accessible and use it, following the example of successful projects such as Edible Islington and the London Orchard Project.

Implementation: Islington Council engaged 40 residents' groups on 40 estates to reclaim disused space for public use. This included the reclamation of an unused patch of land on the Spring Gardens Estate to build a new mini-football pitch there for the community to use and the setting up of community gardens on the Harvist Estate. On the same theme, the council has built Bunhill Heat and Power Station, which provides cleaner, cheaper heat for a swimming pool, a leisure centre and two estates. The next phase of this project will see the power plant deriving energy from waste heat from the Northern Line of the Tube below. The council also made Islington London's first 20-miles-per-hour borough on all but Transport for London's roads, and other local authorities in London and elsewhere are now following suit.

SAFETY

RECOMMENDATION 12: ANTISOCIAL BEHAVIOUR

Antisocial behaviour damages communities and contributes to social isolation.

A single telephone number should be established for reporting antisocial behaviour, requiring collaboration between housing associations, Homes for Islington, Islington Police, and the council. This should improve residents' experience when reporting antisocial behaviour and simplify the route to getting concerns addressed. The resulting coordinated response should enable a more effective and efficient approach to tackling antisocial behaviour, particularly on estates.

Implementation: The council set up a single 24/7 antisocial behaviour hotline with a coordinated response capability across departments such as noise patrol, community safety, Parkguard, and estate management, which now receives in excess of a thousand calls a month. The council also invested £2 million in upgrading its CCTV coverage and systems.

Recommendation 13: Fallout from crime

Tackling crime is about more than just punishing its perpetrators.

Islington Council, together with its partners in victim support and Islington Police's Safer Neighbourhoods teams, should enhance the work done with individuals and communities that are victims of crime and antisocial behaviour to resolve local problems. This should include further work to implement restorative justice, acceptable behaviour contracts, community payback and reparation, and the return of the proceeds of crime.

Implementation: Islington became a London pilot area for neighbourhood resolution panels. The council has invested an additional £500,000 per annum for four years from 2016/17 in targeted support for vulnerable young people at risk of getting drawn into criminality and gangs. Islington has published a strategy for 2017–21 for tackling violence against women and girls, which explicitly recognises that children who experience or witness domestic violence in the home are much more likely to fall victim to it – or perpetrate it – themselves in later life. The council and its partners appreciate that the line between victims and perpetrators is often blurred and that the most punitive sanctions for criminal behaviour are rarely the most rehabilitative.

HOUSING

Recommendation 14: Overcrowding

Tackling overcrowding needs to be a top priority in Islington.

Planning policies and the council's new-build programme should prefer family-sized housing.

Tenancy audits should continue to establish the potential for downsizing.

Islington Council should do even more to enhance its offer to underoccupiers of more appropriately-sized accommodation. This could include three-way swaps, holding local swap meetings, ensuring a move happens within a year, getting people who have downsized to speak to people who are eligible to do so about the benefits, and offering a tailored package of support to help older people downsize from properties they can no longer manage (while making clear to those who may be concerned that evictions and forced transfers on these grounds are out of the question).

Each year, the council should estimate the maximum potential number of underoccupation moves, based on the supply of smaller homes, and provide incentives and support to reach this maximum.

Reviews of allocation policies and lettings processes should ensure that priority for overcrowding is maintained, and where possible increased.

Implementation: Islington Council introduced a rent-guarantee scheme for downsizing tenants. Most of the flats the council builds are family units. The council's allocations policy has been renewed, maintaining its focus on need as the primary criterion. A full review of the council's stock takes place regularly to identify any properties with potential for downsizing or acute problems with overcrowding.

RECOMMENDATION 15: HOUSING SUPPLY

Increasing the supply of decent, genuinely affordable homes is essential.

Islington Council should strive to bring empty space into residential use by:

- eliminating empty space above shops by writing to all shop owners to discuss the opportunities and benefits of using this space, and requiring relevant staff (e.g. town centre managers, Trading Standards officers and Environmental Health officers) to enquire about space above shops as a matter of routine
- identifying empty space in commercial and office buildings for conversion for residential use, especially properties that have remained empty for some time and those that are in residential rather than commercial areas.

The council and housing associations should maximise their efforts to eliminate housing fraud and illegal subletting, so that social housing is used fairly, according to need.

The council should work with housing associations to ensure a supply of genuinely affordable social housing and discourage rent levels that are out of reach of people on average or low incomes.

Implementation: Islington saw over 2,000 genuinely affordable (i.e. at the level of social rent) properties built between 2011 and 2015 – one of the most intensive new-build programmes in the country, despite Islington already being the most densely populated borough in the UK. The council's local lettings policy means that existing tenants have the first option to move into newly built council properties on their estate. An audit was performed by the council of empty properties in the borough, and these are steadily being brought back into use. Anti-fraud campaigns are seeing illegally sublet properties repossessed.

HEALTH

RECOMMENDATION 16: HEALTH INEQUALITIES
Islington's stark health inequalities demand a more active and targeted response.

The new Health and Wellbeing Board should draw up a clear plan of action to address well-documented health inequalities in the borough. This plan should include targeted responses to populations in need, including preventative programmes tailored to the needs of deprived or excluded groups, such as people with learning difficulties or serious mental health problems, homeless people and older people.

Implementation: Those at increased risk of cardiovascular disease in Islington are being prioritised for NHS health checks. Bowel- and lung-cancer awareness sessions are being delivered in the most deprived areas of the borough.

RECOMMENDATION 17: CHILDREN'S HEALTH
Good health in childhood is essential to a fairer Islington.

NHS Islington and Islington Council should:
- support all schools in Islington to achieve Enhanced Healthy Schools status and all children's centres to achieve Healthy Children's Centre status
- ensure every child has free vitamin drops up to the age of five
- undertake an inequalities analysis of immunisation uptake,

to ensure that effort to support this programme is adequately targeted

- seek to reduce the number (or at least check the further proliferation) of fast-food outlets near schools.

Implementation: Islington has increased its numbers of Healthy Children's Centres, Healthy Schools and Enhanced Healthy Schools. Most importantly, the council introduced free school meals for all Islington primary school children, improving behaviour and education and reducing parental costs and stigma. In 2016 the council also passed a new supplementary planning document limiting the proliferation of fast-food outlets in areas of overconcentration.

RECOMMENDATION 18: MENTAL HEALTH
Times of economic hardship are particularly stressful, so we must increase support for mental health.

NHS Islington needs to increase the number of people with depression and anxiety who are accessing support, particularly with levels of unemployment rising and increasing financial hardship, which will increase mental ill health in the borough.

Implementation: Access to iCope (Islington Council's Improving Access to Psychological Therapies service) is increasing and a series of health equity audits have been conducted to ensure that those who most need to access the service are doing so. Some community-specific initiatives have also taken place (e.g. Making the Most of Relationships sessions with men and Feeling Good groups to tackle social isolation among older people). The council has also recruited mental health champions in workplaces and encouraged the take-up of mental health first aid training.

RECOMMENDATION 19: EXERCISE
Islington's health would improve significantly if more people exercised.

Islington Council should:

- negotiate with the Mayor of London and Transport for London to make it easier to cycle in Islington by getting the Barclays Bikes scheme extended further north into the borough, by en-

couraging people from all backgrounds to use it, and by getting the Freedom Pass and/or other concessions to work on it
- explore with schools, Aqua Terra and other relevant partners how to make it easier for local residents to use the excellent school sporting facilities, including swimming pools, we now have in the borough.

Islington GPs should use to the full their ability to prescribe exercise.

Implementation: Arsenal in the Community has helped Islington Council to deliver exercise on referral from GPs. An exercise programme has also been run for those who have survived cancer. Usage of Islington's leisure centres continues to rise. The sports facilities at Highbury Fields, for example, have been refurbished. Despite the council's urging, Transport for London has proven unwilling to extend what are no longer 'Boris Bikes' but instead 'Sadiq's Cycles' further north into the borough.

Annex B: Study guide

Equality as an article of faith

Questions:
- What motivates you to care about inequality in the world around you?
- How does your Quaker faith inform your perspective on equality?

Challenge:
- How connected (or otherwise) are ideas of equality and diversity, and how diverse is your meeting?

Discussion topic:
- What Quaker sources and examples can we draw upon in figuring out how to approach the challenges posed by inequality in our society and further afield?

Inequality in the UK and the world today

Questions:
- In what forms do you observe inequality around you in the UK today?
- Which are the most and least unequal countries on earth?

Challenge:
- What are the most useful ways to measure or gauge inequality, and why?

Discussion topic:
- Which matters more: inequality within a country or inequality between countries?

Through politics, progress is possible

Questions:
- Have you been involved in a campaign or in activism that made a difference?
- What are the most powerful examples you can think of globally of political action making the world a more equal place?

Challenge:
- Identify and assess the impact of two recent movements that sought to tackle inequality.

Discussion topic:
- Which is more important and why: participatory politics or representative politics?

Communicating effectively about equality

Questions:
- Are tackling poverty and reducing inequality the same thing?
- What are the strengths and weaknesses of the vocabulary we tend to use when discussing issues of equality?

Challenge:
- Identify the most persuasive egalitarian message you have encountered and explain why you found it so compelling.

Discussion topic:
- What are the differences between focusing on equality of opportunity and on equality of outcome?

We can all make the world around us a more equal place

Questions:
- Where does your local authority area rank nationally according to the multiple indices of deprivation?
- What are the most glaring inequalities in evidence where you live?

Challenge:
- Establish which pioneers of equality have a connection with the place where you live or somewhere nearby and identify what they achieved.

Discussion topic:
- Where have you seen or been part of a campaign that has secured change to make a place more equal?

Equality in housing

Questions:
- Where are social housing, privately rented housing and owner-occupied housing concentrated in your area?
- How do the costs of living in each of these three tenures vary locally?

Challenge:
- Find out how many people are on your local authority's waiting list for social housing and how many people in your area are homeless.

Discussion topic:
- What more can you do as individuals and as a meeting to help ensure that everyone in your area has an affordable, secure and decent home?

Equality at work

Questions:
- What are the levels of unemployment and underemployment in your area?
- Which are the big employers in your area and are they accredited Living Wage Employers?

Challenge:
- Try to establish the internal pay ratio at your place of work, your council and your nearest football club. How transparent are they with information on pay?

Discussion topic:
- Does it matter what people get paid at the top of organisations, and why? If it does, what is an ideal ratio for lowest:highest paid within an organisation?

Equality in other fields of public policy

Dealing with debt
Questions:
- What levels of interest are charged by payday lenders, by credit unions and by banks in your area?
- What sort of crisis in your life might tip you over the edge of unmanageable debt?

Challenge:
- Find out what you can about levels of problem debt in your area, for instance by talking to relevant local charities, advice agencies, housing providers and your local authority. Is it a problem confined to a particular subsection of the local community, or does it cut across such divides?

Discussion topic:
- How can we foster financial literacy and resilience in our area to reduce levels of problem debt?

Equal from the start
Questions:
- Is there childcare provision within pram-pushing distance for everyone in your area? How much does it cost?
- What proportion of schoolchildren in your area receive free school meals, and how do they fare in attainment terms compared with their peers?

Challenge:
- Find out what you can about child poverty in your area, broken down geographically and demographically. Then consider what its effects are and what you can do to help address it.

Discussion topic:
- How real is equality of opportunity for young people in your area? What can you do to level the playing field?

Equally safe and secure
Questions:
- Is hate crime an issue in your community? Who tend to be its victims? How often are the perpetrators caught and convicted?
- How many Syrian refugees have settled in your area since the war in Syria broke out?

Challenge:
- Consider how you and others in your meeting might look to engage with those responsible for hate crime to limit its future occurrence.

Discussion topic:
- How should we balance the needs of refugees with the needs of existing residents? How should this inform decisions about precious resources such as housing?

Equality as both end and means

Questions:
- What is the level of political engagement in your area, for instance in political parties, in single-issue campaigns, in voter turnout, and so on?
- How politically engaged are you?

Challenge:
- Identify a local campaign you could join or set up that would help to make your area more equal.

Discussion topic:
- How could your meeting contribute more to political life locally in order to help make your area a more equal place?